Dr. Seuss Workbook
HANDWRITING

There are few things as fun as the fabulous thrill of learning and using a brand-new skill!

Welcome to Dr. Seuss Workbooks, where kids learn and practice important skills they'll use in the classroom and beyond! Grab a pencil and get ready to explore handwriting.

For the best results, spend time with your child practicing the correct way to hold a pencil.

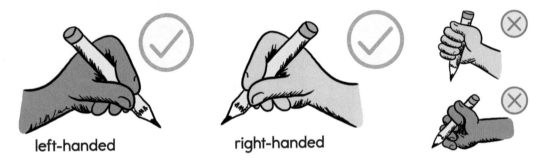

left-handed   right-handed

Help your child become familiar with our "dot and arrow" steps to write letters and numbers.

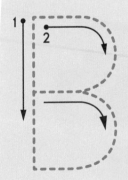

Each black dot (•) indicates the beginning of a new line, where the pencil should leave the page to make a separate stroke. The arrows (→) show the direction of pencil movement. Strokes without numbers indicate a continuation and change of direction.

We hope your child will learn, laugh, and build confidence on the road to becoming a lifelong learner!

—Your friends at Dr. Seuss

Get ready to write letters by tracing these lines.
Start at each dot and follow the arrows without
lifting your hand.

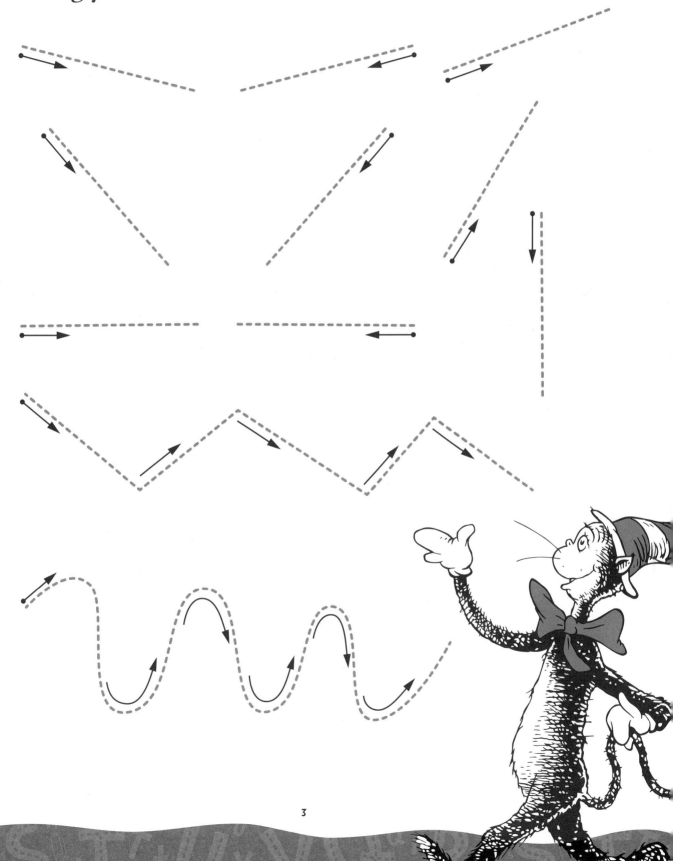

Practice the Steps

Trace each line. Then draw it again by yourself.

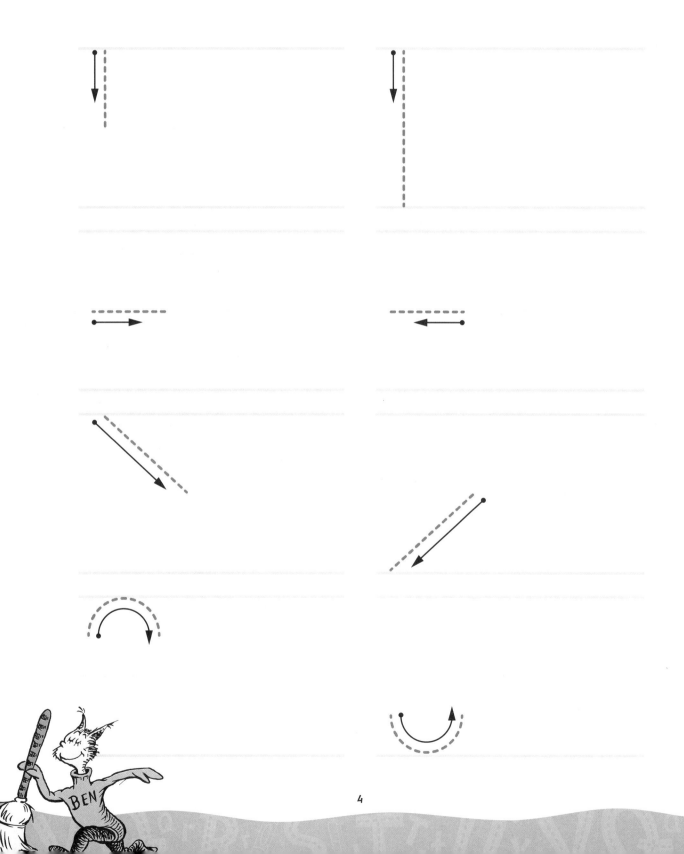

Trace each line or shape, then draw it again.
Start at dots with the number 1 and follow the
direction of the arrows. If you see a new number,
pick up your pencil and start a new line.

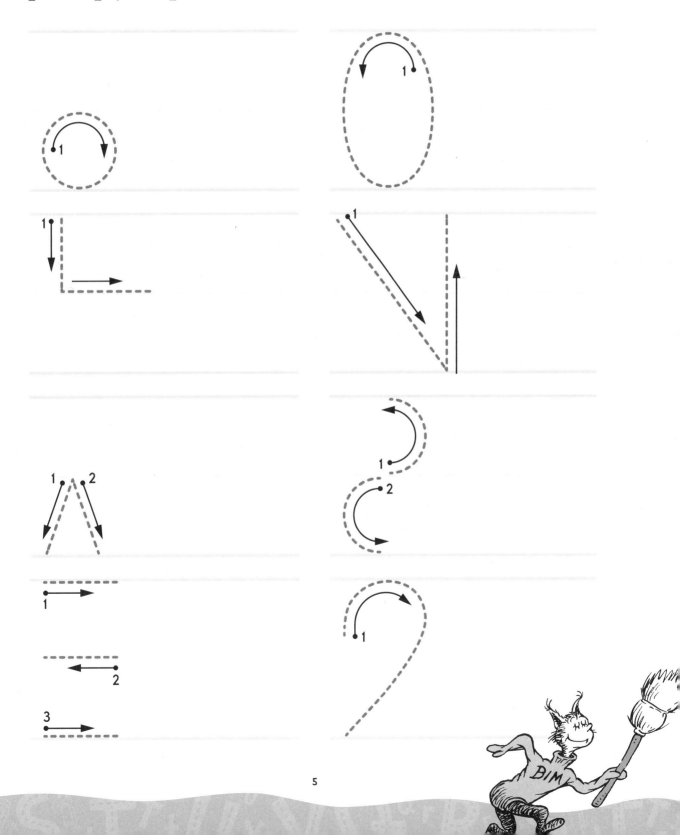

The Letter A

BIG

little

apple

Trace big letter A.

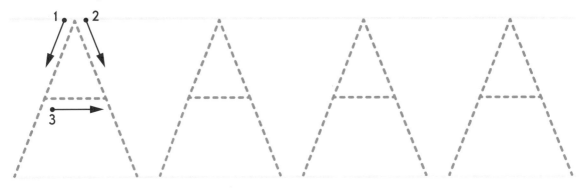

Write big letter A.

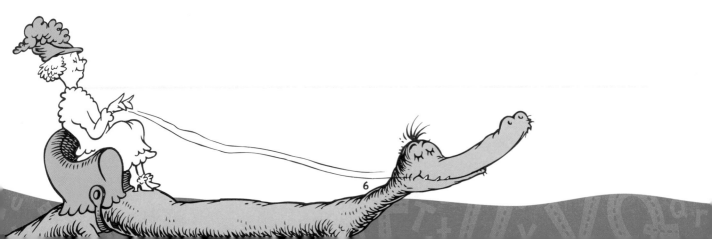

Trace little letter **a**.

Write little letter **a**.

Write **a** to complete each word.

h _ t c _ t f _ n

The Letter B

BIG   little

book

Trace big letter **B**.

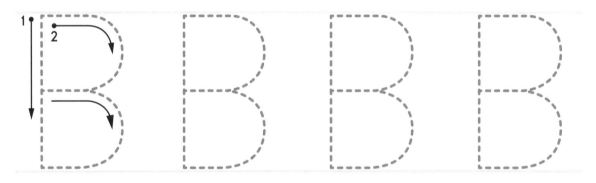

Write big letter **B**.

Trace little letter **b**.

Write little letter **b**.

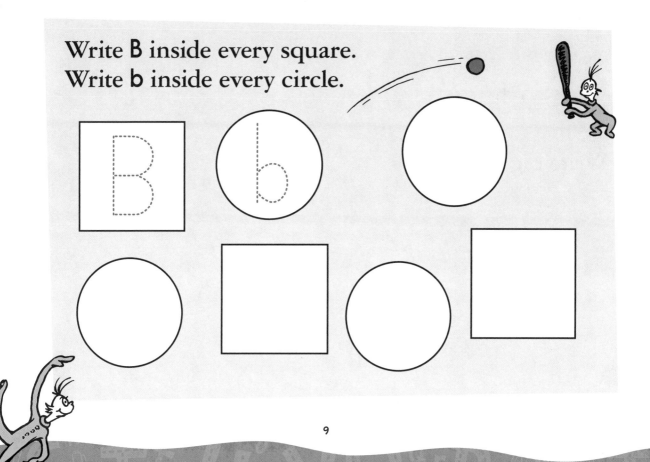

Write **B** inside every square.
Write **b** inside every circle.

The Letter C

BIG

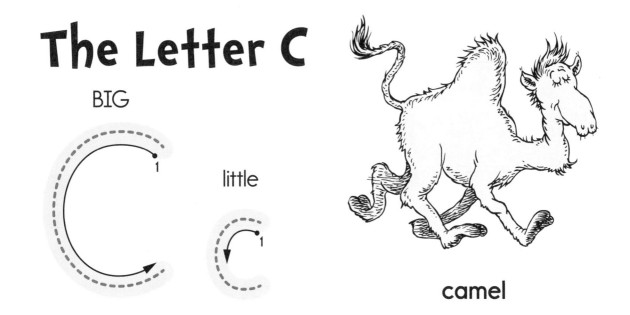

little

camel

Trace big letter C.

Write big letter C.

Trace little letter c.

C C C C C

Write little letter c.

Trace each letter that is a C or c.

C R g C c

k c C c m

k C C c

c C c

The Letter D

BIG   little

dog

Trace big letter D.

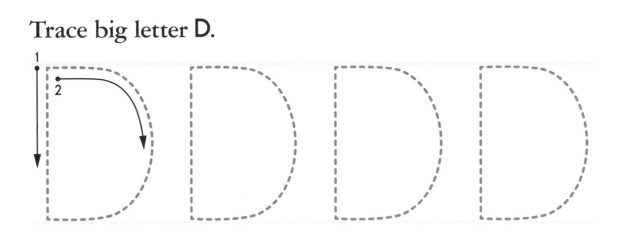

Write big letter D.

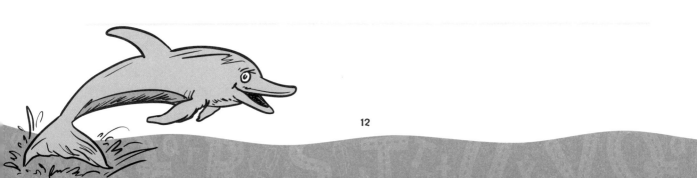

Trace little letter **d**.

Write little letter **d**.

Trace **D** or **d** on each door.

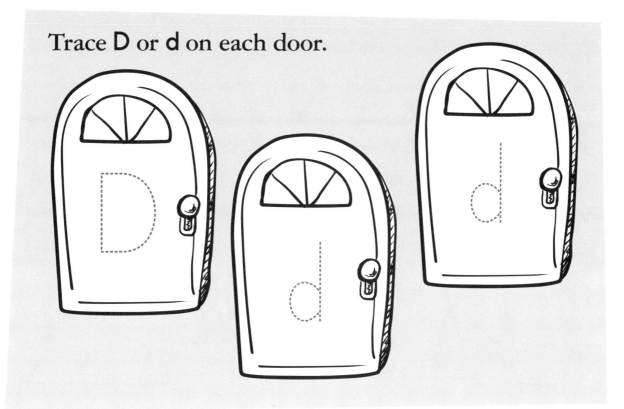

You're Getting Better with Letters!

Trace the letter in each shape. Then draw lines to connect the shapes with matching big and little letters.

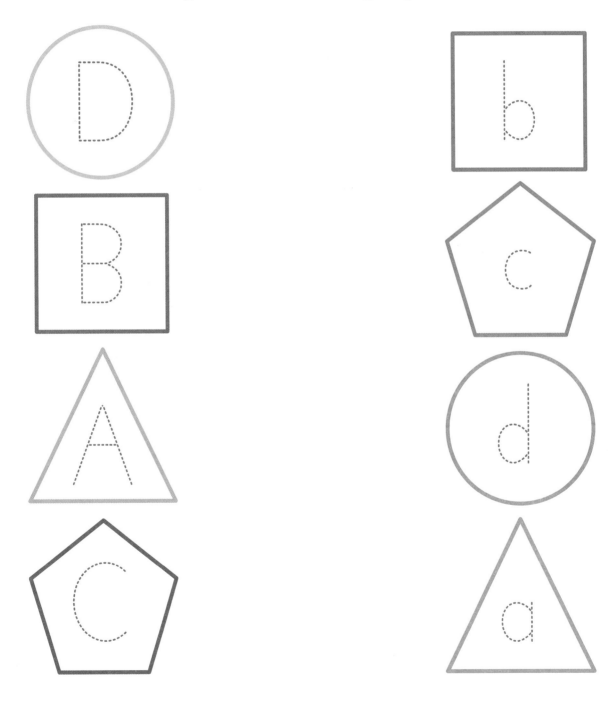

Trace the missing letters to finish each word.

bat car dice

duck bed can

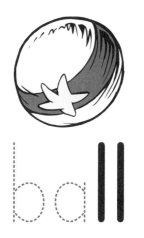

ball crab baby

The Letter E

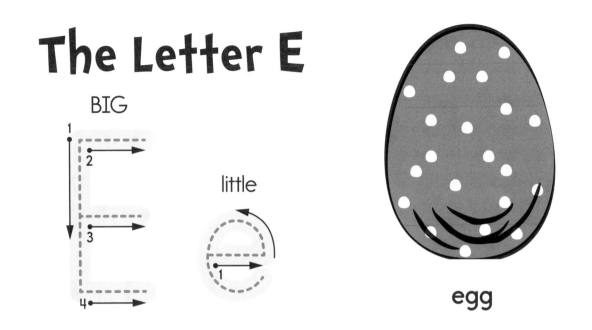

BIG

little

egg

Trace big letter E.

Write big letter E.

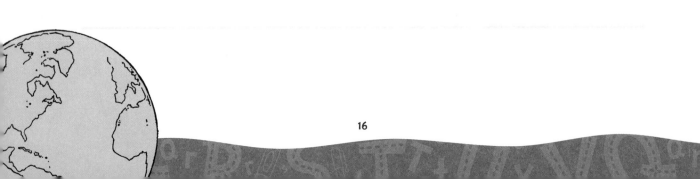

Trace little letter **e**.

Write little letter **e**.

Write **e** to complete each word.

p__t n__t b__d

The Letter F

BIG   little

fly

Trace big letter **F**.

Write big letter **F**.

Trace little letter f.

f f f f f

Write little letter f.

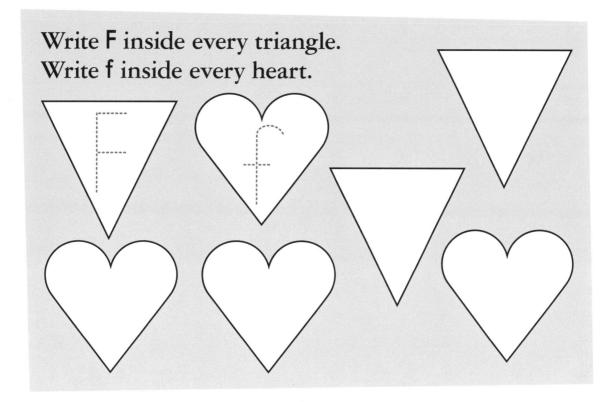

Write **F** inside every triangle.
Write **f** inside every heart.

The Letter G

BIG

little

goat

Trace big letter **G**.

Write big letter **G**.

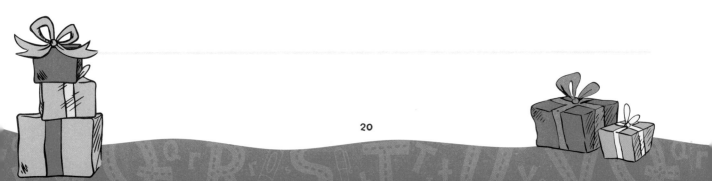

Trace little letter **g**.

Write little letter **g**.

Trace each letter that is a **G** or **g**.

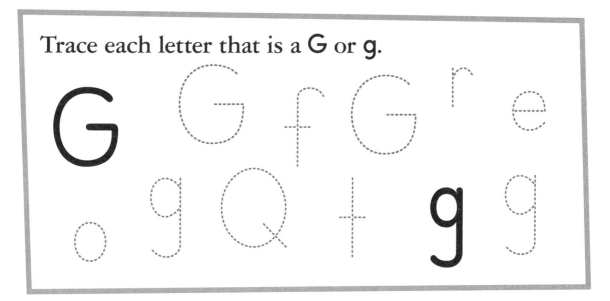

The Letter H

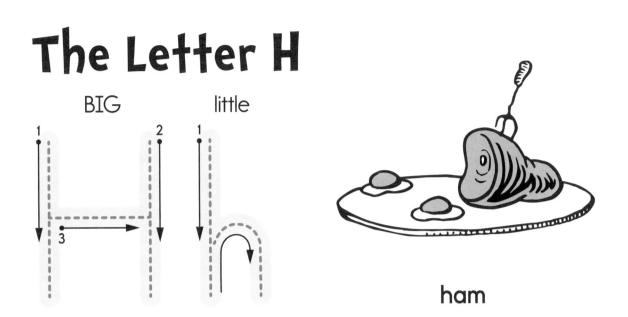

BIG   little

ham

Trace big letter H.

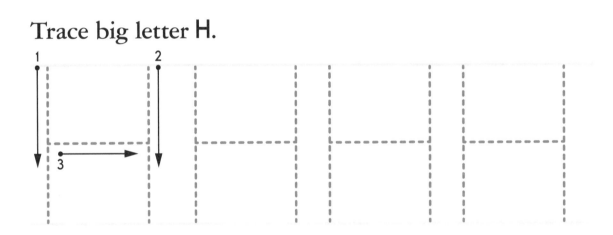

Write big letter H.

Trace little letter h.

Write little letter h.

Trace H or h on each hat.

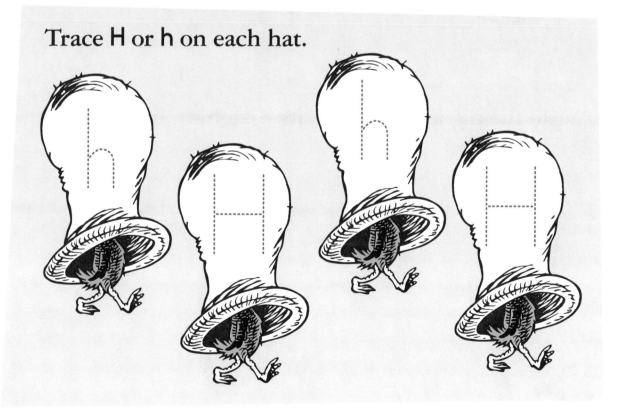

You Can Write, All Right!

Write the little letter next to its matching big letter.

E

F

G

H

Write the big letter next to its matching little letter.

h

g

Trace the missing letters to finish each word.

dress   fish   grass

hair   bath   bean

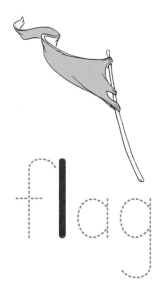

flag   dog   grapes

Letter Go!

Circle every letter
that you find in this
picture. Then write
each letter on one of
the spaces provided.

d

b

G

D

g

h

THING 2

THING 1

27

The Letter I

BIG

little

ice

Trace big letter I.

Write big letter I.

Trace little letter i.

.2

1

Write little letter i.

Write i to complete each word.

t__e   z__p   p__n

The Letter J

BIG

little

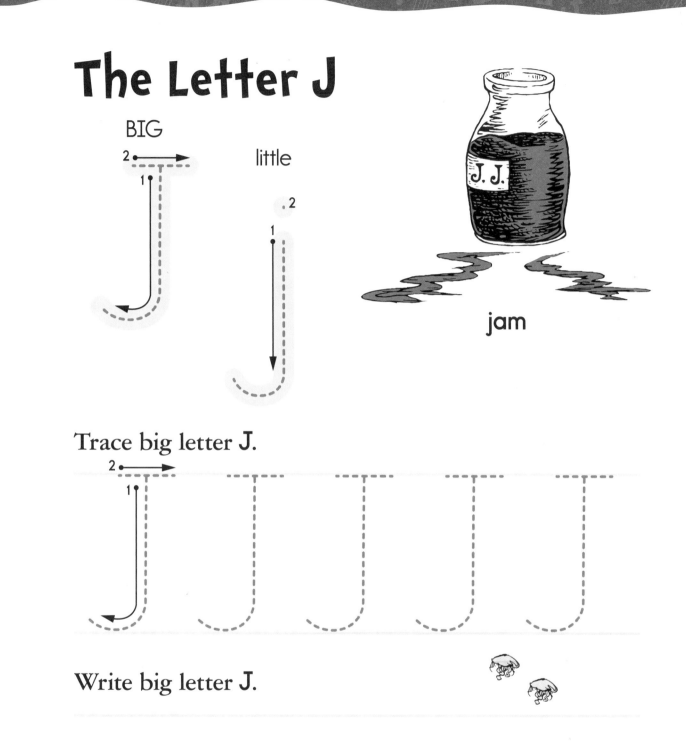

jam

Trace big letter **J**.

Write big letter **J**.

Trace little letter j.

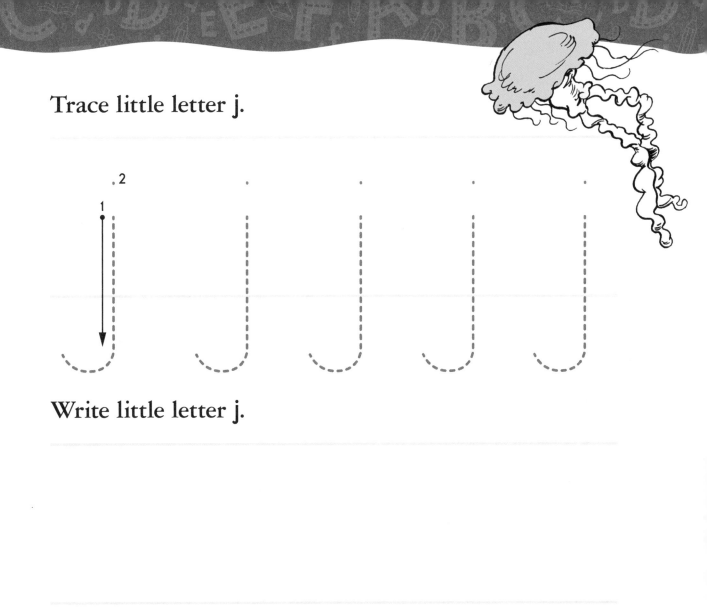

Write little letter j.

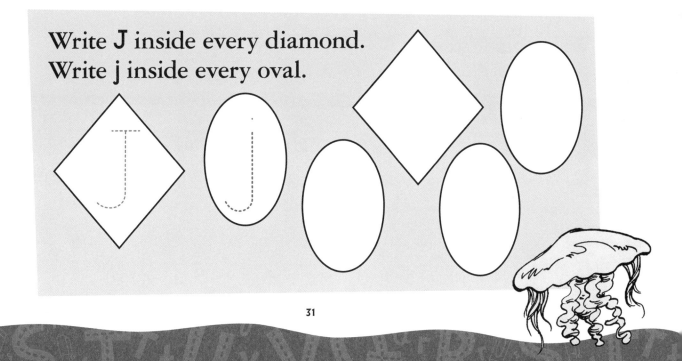

Write **J** inside every diamond.
Write j inside every oval.

The Letter K

BIG   little

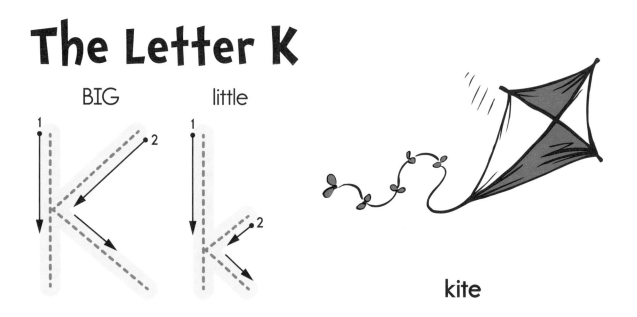

kite

Trace big letter K.

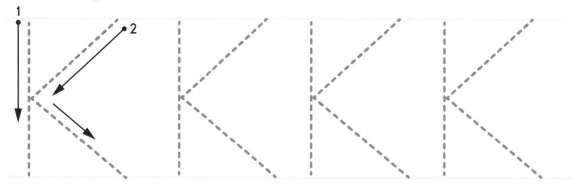

Write big letter K.

Trace little letter k.

Write little letter k.

Trace each letter that is a K or k.

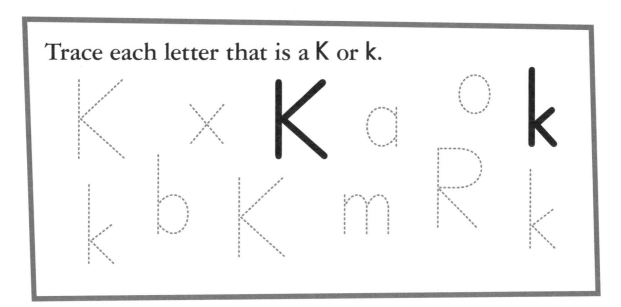

The Letter L

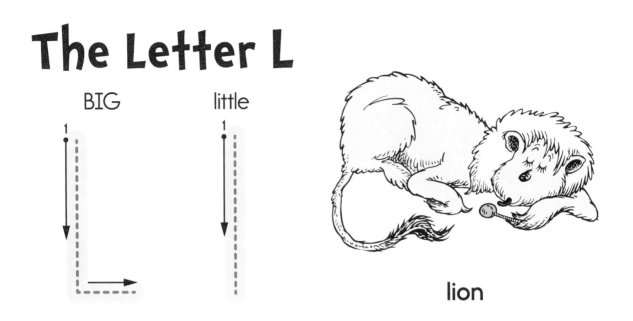

BIG   little

lion

Trace big letter L.

Write big letter L.

Trace little letter l.

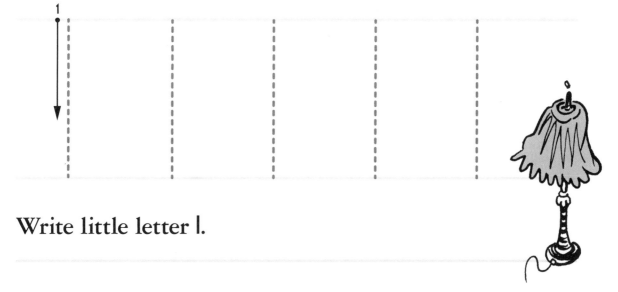

Write little letter l.

Trace L or l on each lemon.

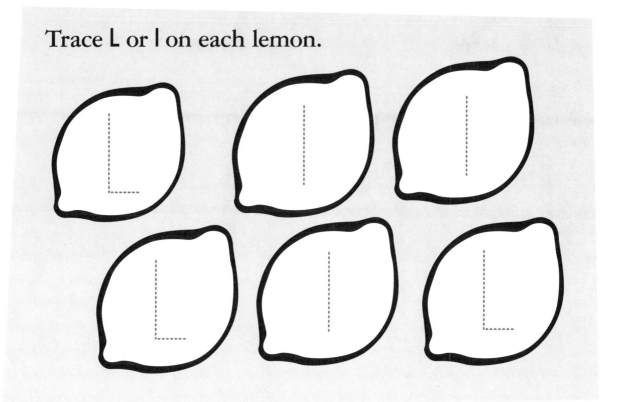

Oh, the Letters You Know!

Write the little letter next to its matching big letter.

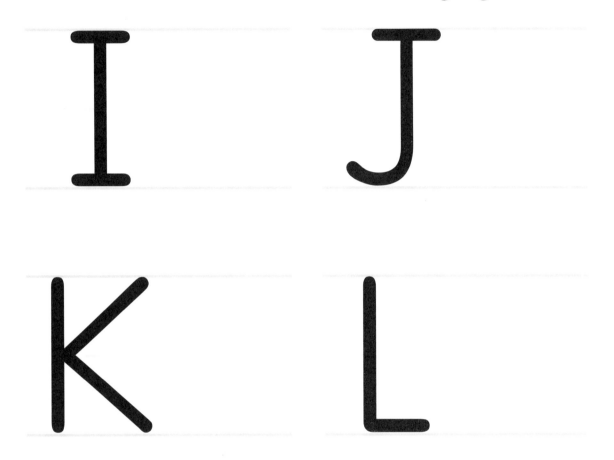

Write the big letter next to its matching little letter.

Trace the missing letters in each word.

bike   jar   ball

leaf   book   bird

  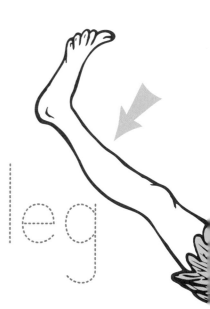

brick   milk   leg

The Letter M

BIG

little

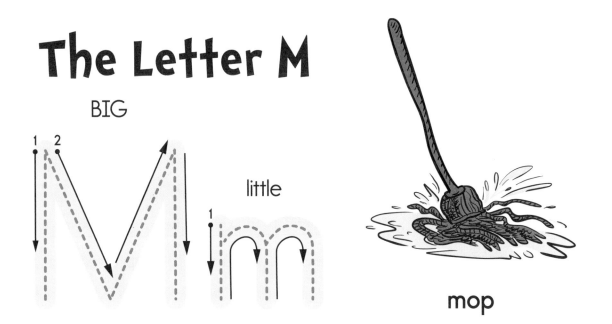

mop

Trace big letter M.

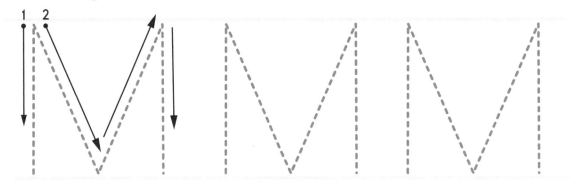

Write big letter M.

38

Trace little letter **m**.

Write little letter **m**.

Write **m** to complete each word.

_it   ja_   di_e

The Letter N

BIG

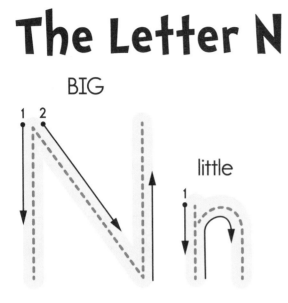

little

nest

Trace big letter N.

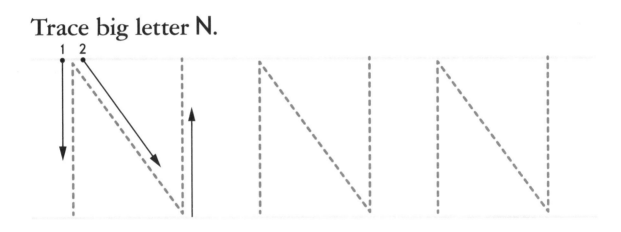

Write big letter N.

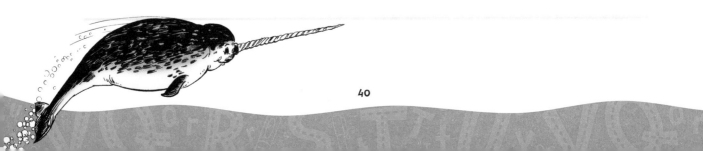

Trace little letter n.

Write little letter n.

Write N inside every square.
Write n inside every circle.

The Letter O

BIG

little

owl

Trace big letter O.

Write big letter O.

Trace little letter o.

Write little letter o.

Trace each letter that is an O or o.

The Letter P

BIG

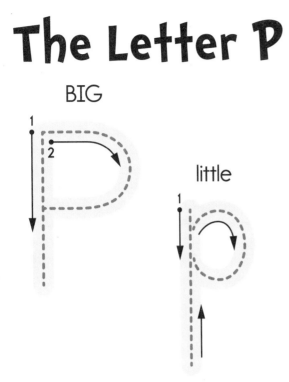

little

pig

Trace big letter P.

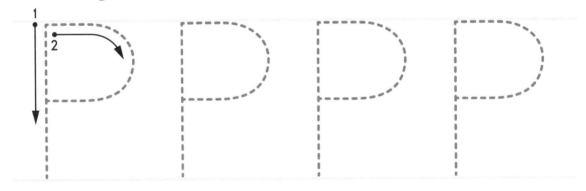

Write big letter P.

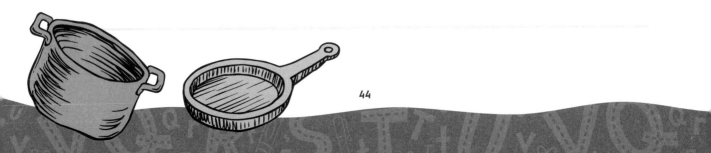

Trace little letter p.

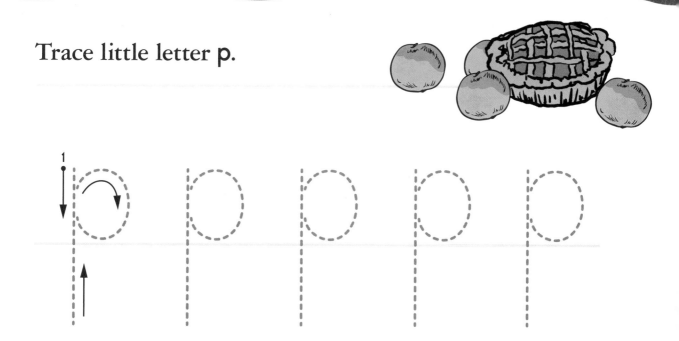

Write little letter p.

Trace **P** or **p** on each pepper.

I know M, N, O, and P!

Write the little letter next to its matching big letter.

M   N

O   P

Write the big letter next to its matching little letter.

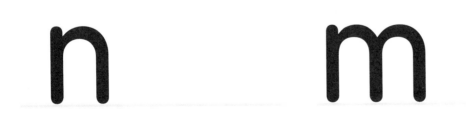

n   m

Trace the missing letters in each word.

gem   ant   mice

pan   money   top

lime   banana   cup

Amazing Letters

Draw a path from **A** to **P** in order. Then go back and trace all the letters along the path.

Little Letters Everywhere

Trace all the little letters. Then draw lines to connect
them to their matching big letters.

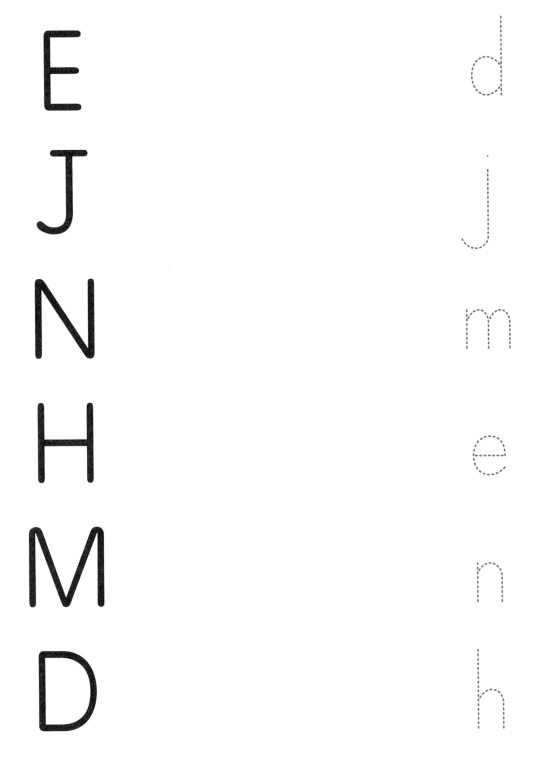

E

J

N

H

M

D

d

j

m

e

n

h

K

G

A

B

L

P

F

f

k

p

l

b

a

g

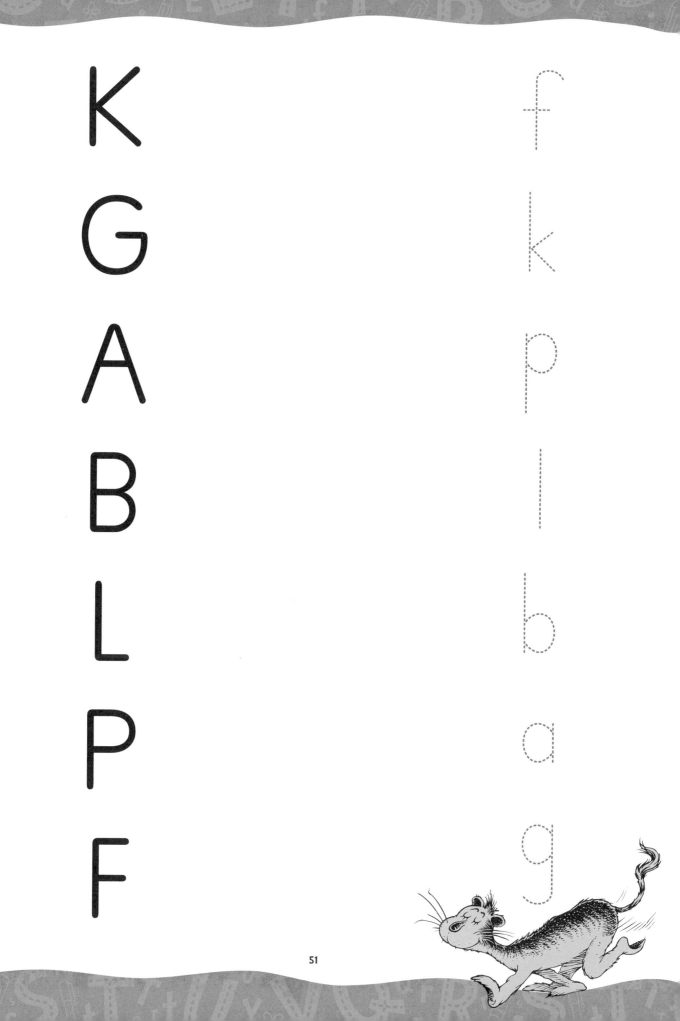

The Letter Q

BIG

little

queen

Trace big letter **Q**.

Write big letter **Q**.

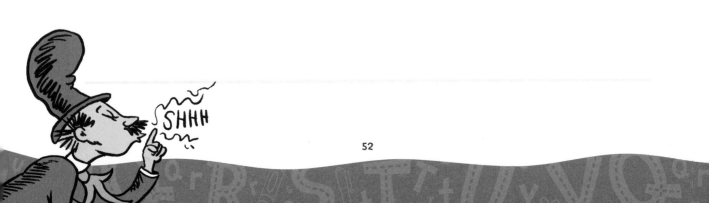

Trace little letter q.

Write little letter q.

Write q to complete each word.

__uilt   __uarter

The Letter R

BIG

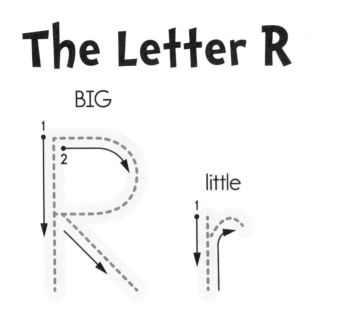

little

reindeer

Trace big letter **R**.

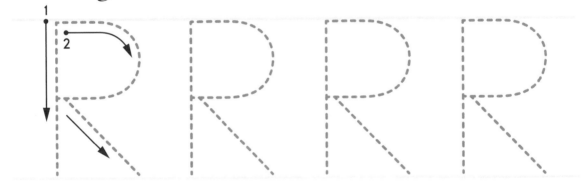

Write big letter **R**.

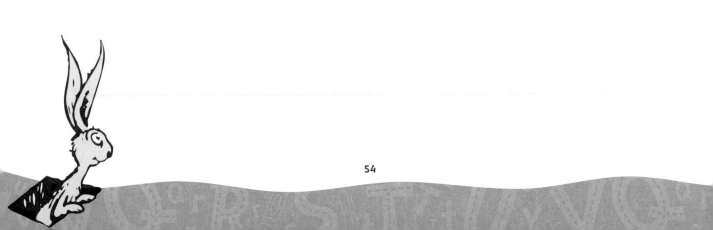

Trace little letter r.

r r r r r

Write little letter r.

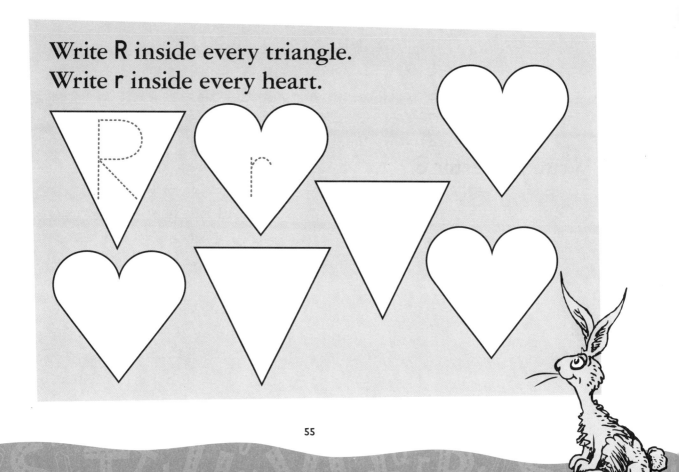

Write **R** inside every triangle.
Write **r** inside every heart.

The Letter S

BIG

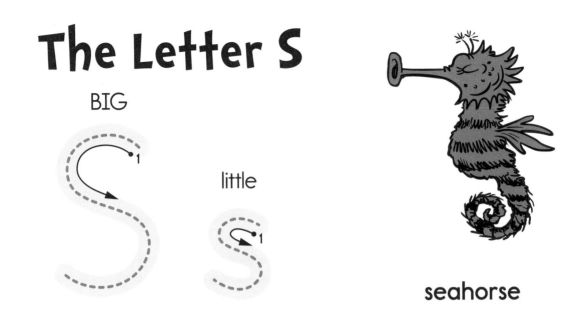

little

seahorse

Trace big letter **S**.

Write big letter **S**.

Trace little letter **s**.

Write little letter **s**.

Trace each letter that is an **S** or **s**.

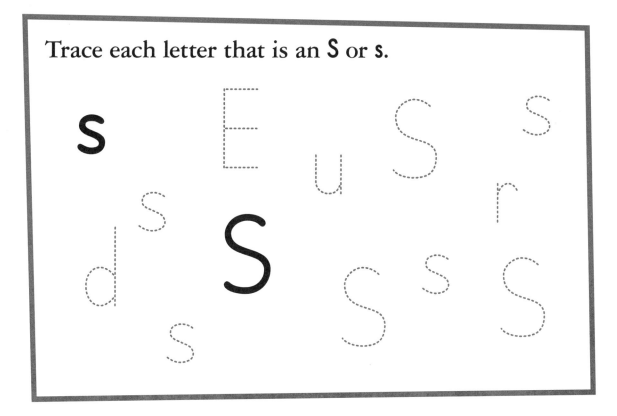

The Letter T

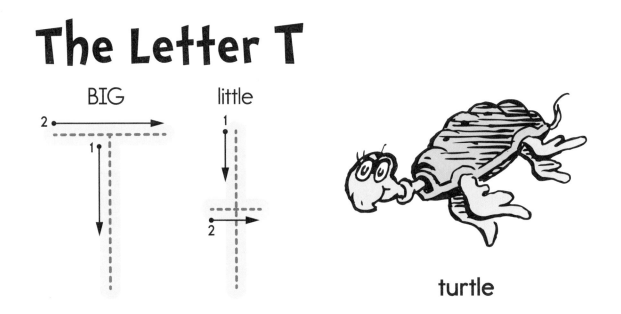

BIG   little

turtle

Trace big letter T.

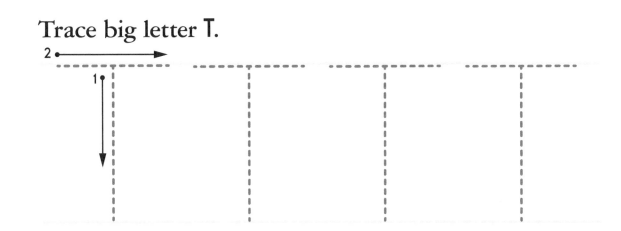

Write big letter T.

Trace little letter t.

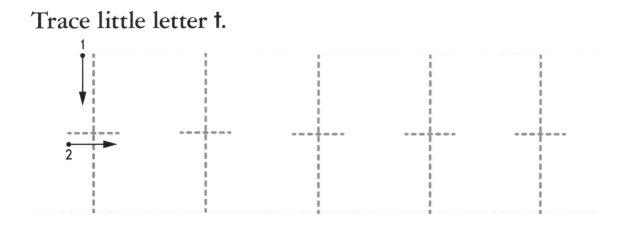

Write little letter t.

Trace T or t on each tomato.

Write All Day and Night!

Write the little letter next to its matching big letter.

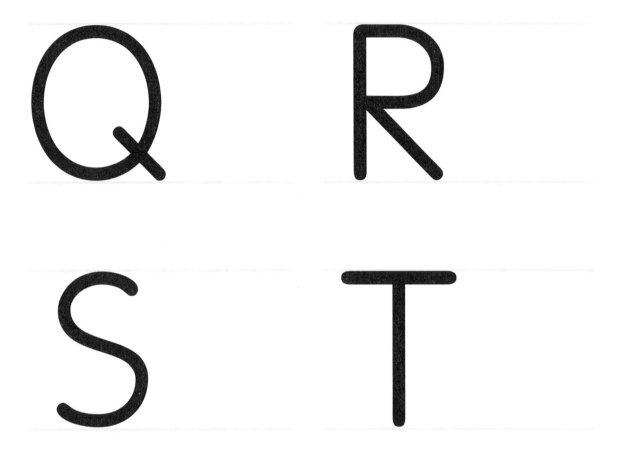

Q

R

S

T

Write the big letter next to its matching little letter.

t

q

Trace the missing letters in each word.

quill   rake   fruit

pot   cheese   list

ski   pants   rose

The Letter U

BIG

little

umbrella

Trace big letter U.

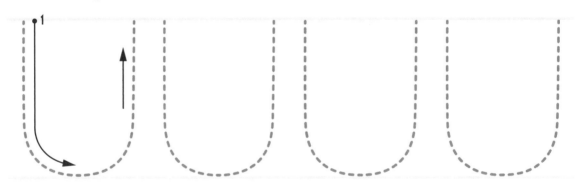

Write big letter U.

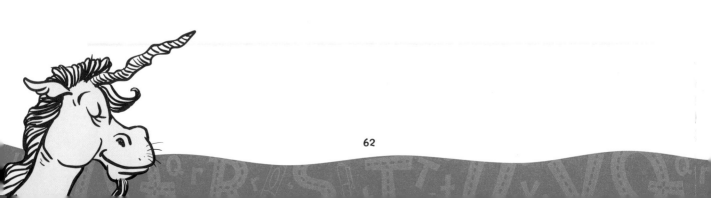

Trace little letter u.

Write little letter u.

Write u to complete each word.

gl__e   b__g   clo__d

The Letter V

BIG

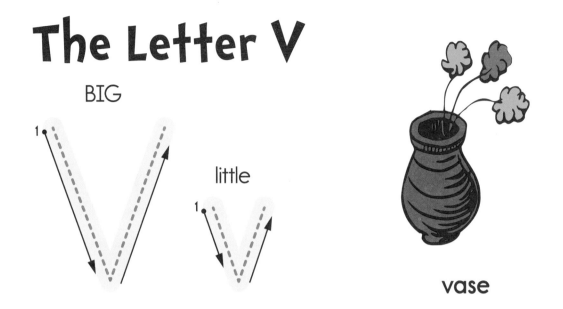

little

vase

Trace big letter V.

Write big letter V.

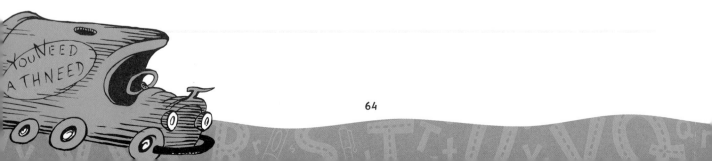

Trace little letter v.

Write little letter v.

Write V inside every square.
Write v inside every circle.

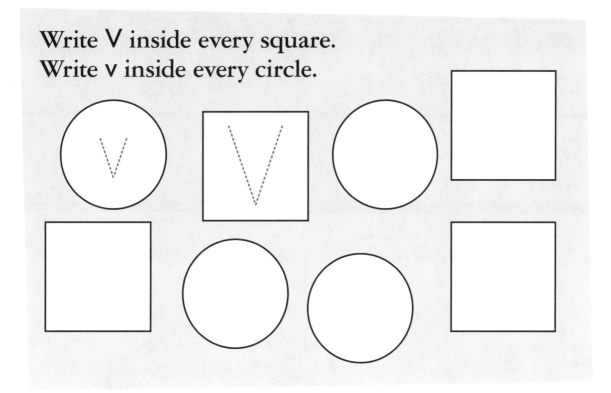

The Letter W

BIG

little

walrus

Trace big letter W.

Write big letter W.

Trace little letter **w**.

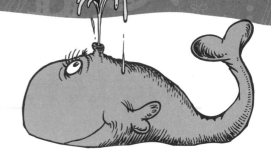

Write little letter **w**.

Trace **W** or **w** in each wreath.

The Letter X

BIG

little

X-ray

Trace big letter **X**.

Write big letter **X**.

Trace little letter **x**.

Write little letter **x**.

Trace each letter that is an **X** or **x**.

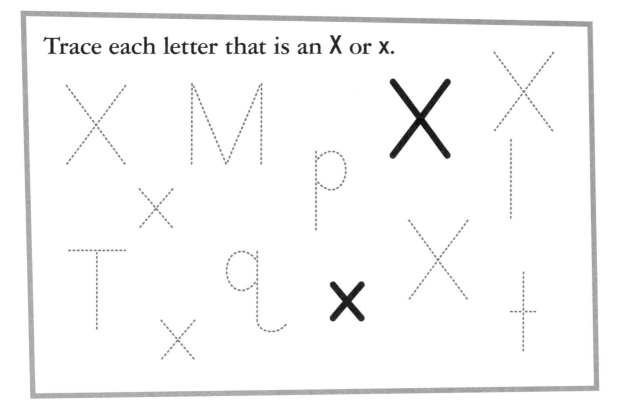

We Love Letters!

Write the little letter next to its matching big letter.

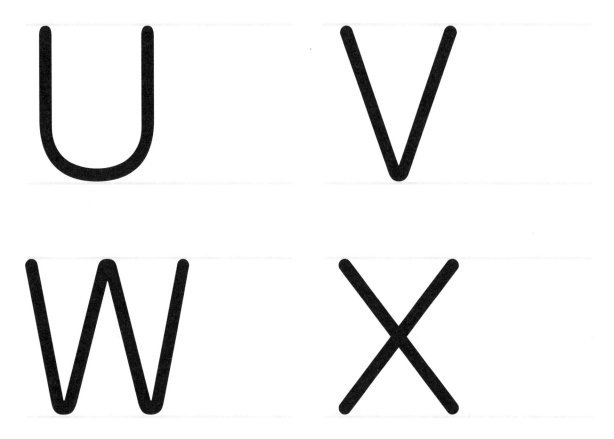

Write the big letter next to its matching little letter.

Trace the letters in each word.

 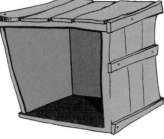 

slug   box   bowl

hive   vase   fox

wig   axe   bush

The Letter Y

BIG

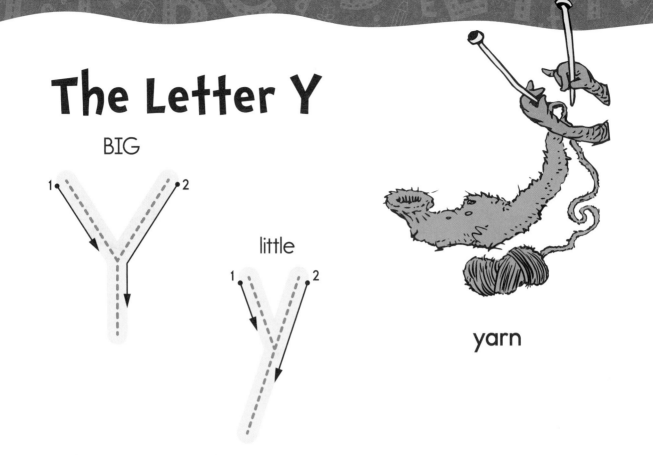

little

yarn

Trace big letter Y.

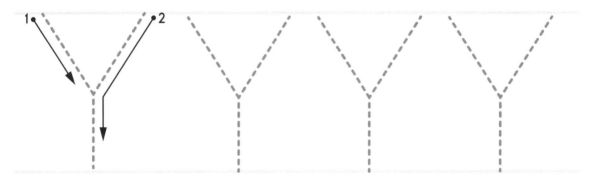

Write big letter Y.

Trace little letter y.

Write little letter y.

Trace each letter that is a **Y** or **y**.

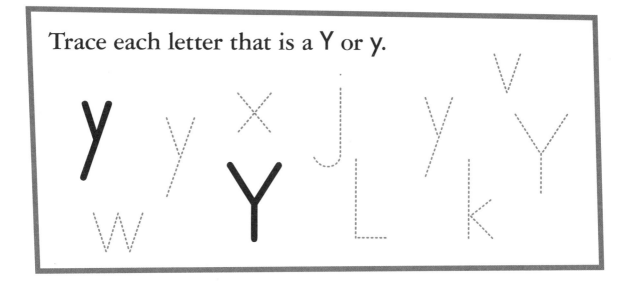

The Letter Z

BIG

little

zebra

Trace big letter **Z**.

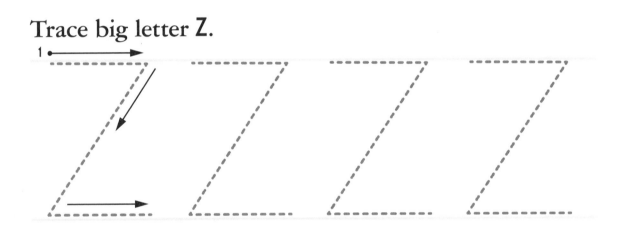

Write big letter **Z**.

Trace little letter **z**.

Write little letter **z**.

Write **Z** inside every oval.
Write **z** inside every diamond.

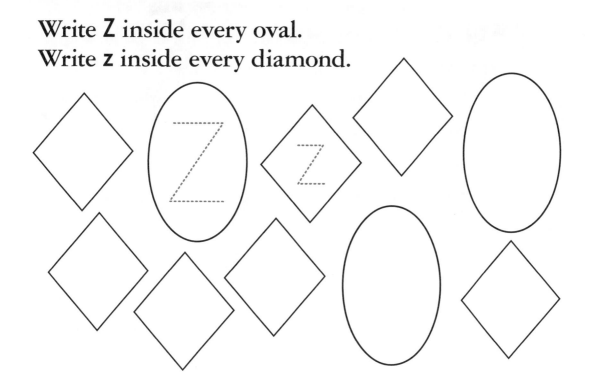

Writing Road

Draw a path from **Q** to **Z** in order. Then go back and trace all the letters along the path.

Look Out for Little Letters

Trace all the little letters. Then draw lines to connect them to their matching big letters.

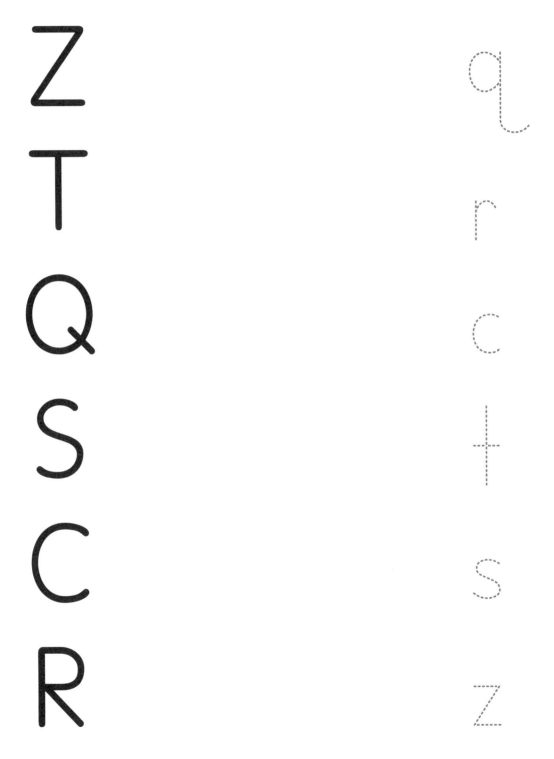

X

U

Y

I

W

O

V

W

i

y

o

x

v

u

The Numbers 1 and 2

Trace the number 1.

Write the number 1.

Trace the number **2**.

Write the number **2**.

Write **1** inside every square.
Write **2** inside every circle.

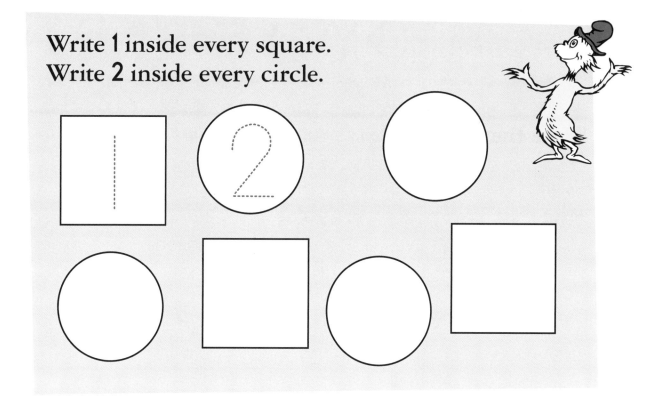

The Numbers 3 and 4

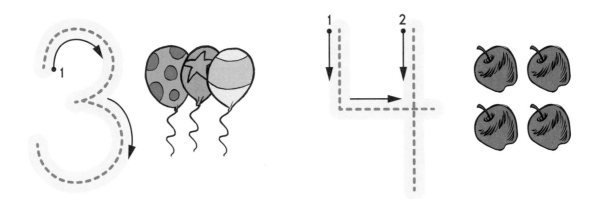

Trace the number **3**.

Write the number **3**.

Trace the number 4.

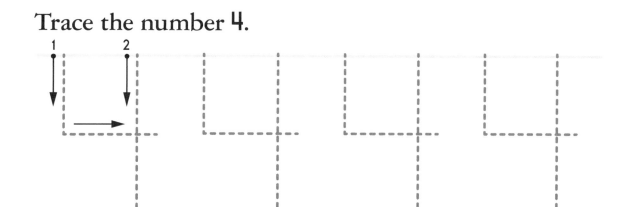

Write the number 4.

Trace each number that is a **3** or **4**.

The Numbers 5 and 6

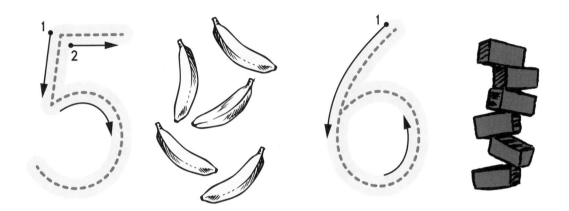

Trace the number **5**.

Write the number **5**.

Trace the number **6**.

Write the number **6**.

Write **5** inside every oval.
Write **6** inside every diamond.

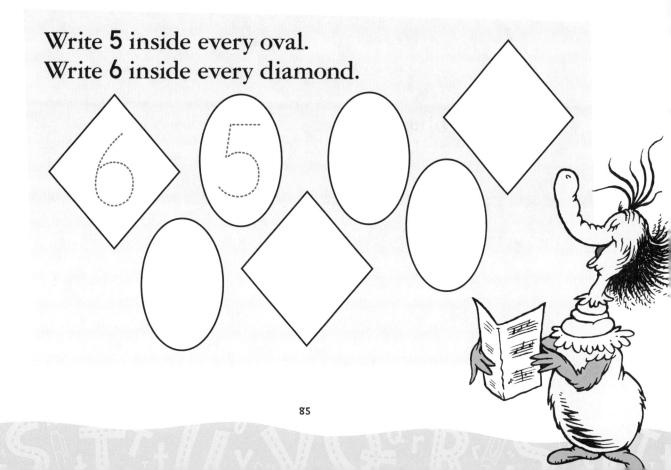

The Numbers 7 and 8

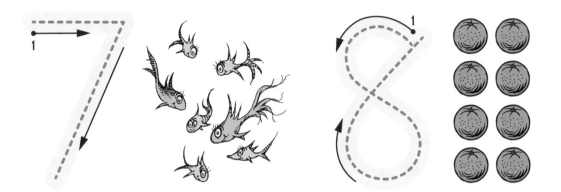

Trace the number **7.**

Write the number **7.**

Trace the number **8**.

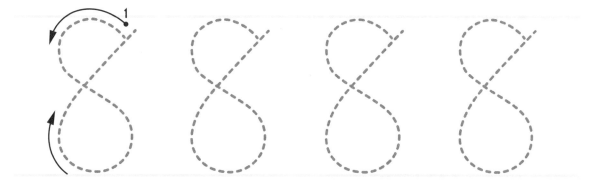

Write the number **8**.

Trace each number that is a **7** or **8**.

The Numbers 9 and 0

Trace the number 9.

Write the number 9.

Trace the number 0.

Write the number 0.

Write 9 inside every triangle.
Write 0 inside every heart.

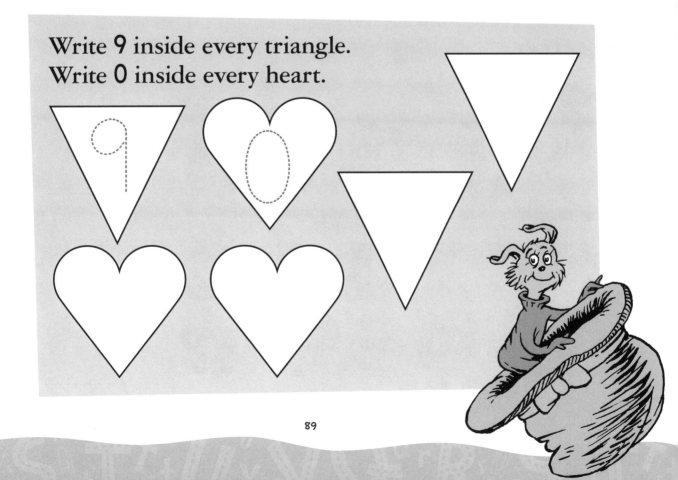

Numbers Count!

Write the correct number next to each group of cookies.

_____

_____

_____

_____

Write the missing numbers in each trail.

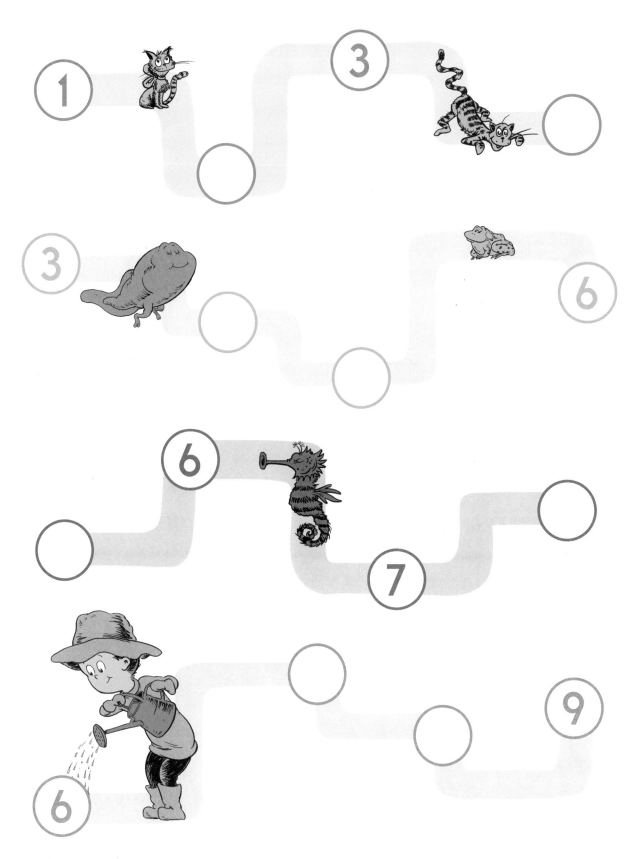

Show What You Know

Trace each group of big and little letters. Then write them again by yourself.

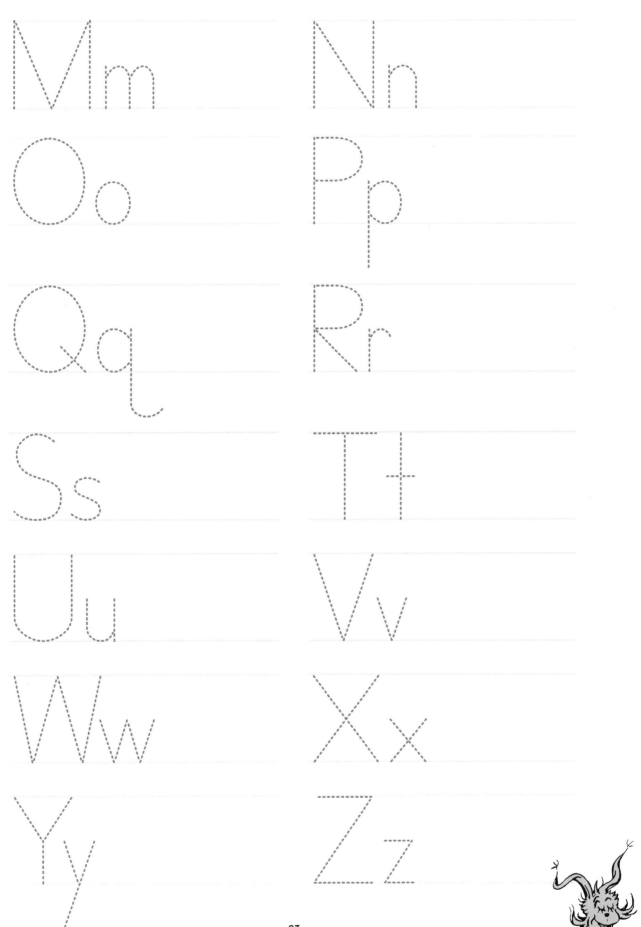

Mm   Nn

Oo   Pp

Qq   Rr

Ss   Tt

Uu   Vv

Ww   Xx

Yy   Zz

What's the Word?

Write the missing letters to complete all the words.
Use the letters in the box to help you.

m	h	t	f	e	w	f
t	r	b	p	o	m	s

Fro_ there to _ere, from
here to _here, _unny
things are _very_here!

One _ish, _wo fish,
_ed fish, _lue fish.

A _erson
is a pers_n
no _atter
how _mall.

94

ANSWERS

Page 14

Pages 26–27

Pages 48–49

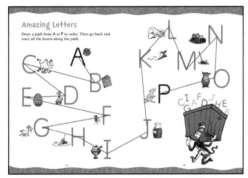

Pages 50–51

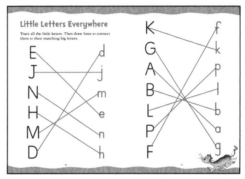

Pages 76–77

Pages 78–79

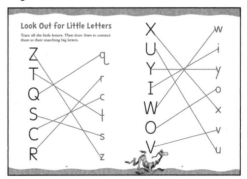

Pages 90–91

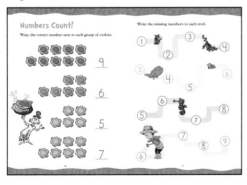

Page 94

HOORAY FOR YOU

**You learned something new.
With this brand-new skill,
there's so much you can do!**

Show off your new skill by writing your name!

NAME

is a

Handwriting Hero!

CERTIFICATE OF ACHIEVEMENT